D1711881

THE PRINCESS WAY

Dedication

The Princess Way is dedicated to Debby Hopkins who is a wonderful model of the Professional Princess.

Acknowledgments

I would like to acknowledge all of my Princess friends for their hard work in becoming a Princess. Without them, I had nothing to write about. I would like to thank my editor, Nancy Porter, who offered counsel regarding perspective on this work. And I would like to thank the Princesses who attend the annual Princess parties for contributing so much of themselves into making the event a life changing experience for so many of us.

Foreword

The title of Princess is not used lightly in this text. Webster's says that a Princess is "a woman considered to have qualities and characteristics of a Princess." What are those qualities and characteristics? Who decides?

My editor, Nancy Porter, asked me what my intention was in writing this book. She was concerned that some of the language in the book might sound overly elitist. My response was that she was entirely accurate. I had intended for the words to reflect an *Attitude*.

Princesses (as they are defined in this text) have *Attitude*. Attitude is one of their most defining characteristics. That Attitude, described in these pages, is critical to breaking through the barriers keeping a woman from all that she wants in the world. This book is about having it all. If a woman does not start with the attitude that she is "worth it," neither will anyone else.

As you read the book, if you find the words or ideas disturbing or reflecting self-indulgence, ask yourself if you would like to be self-indulgent and can't seem to give yourself permission to do so. Ask yourself whose opinion you are worried about and then ask yourself if they have treated you in a way that warrants their potential or presumed judgement of your behavior. Remember this: Princesses are Princesses because they choose to be, not because anyone else has given them permission.

TABLE OF CONTENTS

CHAPTER 1

WHAT IS A PRINCESS?

There is an unnamed but growing movement of women occurring across our planet. It needs a name. The title of Princess is arbitrary. A person could choose any word to describe the women in these pages. Any title would be applicable as long as it described the complete woman who is emerging. She could be called a warrior, a queen, a goddess, or any other name, as long as the name begins to express the larger image contained in this text. You may already have a construct in your mind for the term Princess. Perhaps you will have a new construct after reading *The Princess Way*.

The Princess Way does not just describe a very unique and special woman who is evolving for the first time in history. It also describes her path. Never before have circumstances created the opportunity for such a woman to appear. There are a growing number of women who have worked to understand both the opportunities of such a time and the responsibilities. So who is this woman?

A Princess is a very special person. She is not a person who has attained her status through birth or training, although certainly she may have come from roots where someone, or everyone, confirmed her value and her worth each day. A Princess is not a spoiled and willful child. In fact, bad behavior is very un-Princess-like. A Princess is not a woman with servants and a following of loyal subjects. In fact, true Princesses generally have not lived a life of ease or indulgence.

A true Princess is a woman who has learned to make her own way, often against incredible odds. She has learned the laws of the Universe and she applies them wisely. She has learned the value of humility and she takes nothing for granted. She expects no one to take care of her, for she has learned to take care of herself.

She is strong, not arrogant, flexible rather than brittle. Her loved ones look to her for wisdom rather than service. She serves because she wants to, never because she has to.

Others find her mysterious, funny, warm, generous, or formidable, depending on the circumstance. She is not predictable, because she flows with the Universe rather than living by a predetermined set of rules.

A Princess values herself. She does not need to court others in order to belong. She belongs to herself. Only those who honor her uniqueness and who respect it and nurture it are allowed inside. Others are treated respectfully, but kept at a distance. A Princess knows her own worth and she creates moments and events to honor herself. She needs celebration in her life and she is disciplined about creating opportunities to wallow in her moments of self-appreciation. So many women find that the very concept of self-appreciation produces a deep and disturbing sense of guilt. Princesses don't "do" guilt.

Above all, a Princess is fulfilled. She is aware of her essence and seeks ways to share her gifts and her wisdom. She is emerging as a different style of Leader in a time when her form of Leadership fills an enormous void. The Princess in her fully evolved state integrates an understanding of positional as well as personal power. She is changing organizations and entire cultures with her understandings.

A Princess never allows herself to act as a victim. Although from time to time she may be injured, she is in control of her life and no one is allowed to diminish her potential. She has worked through and made peace with those circumstances and events in her life that she once perceived as blocks to her progress.

A Princess is the creator of her own Universe and she knows it.

CHAPTER 2

A WOMAN IN TRANSITION:
THE PRINCESS JOURNEY

So how does a woman become this wise and powerful creature? Who is eligible and how do they join? Is there a sign-up list?

For most Princesses the moment of decision to become a Princess is not conscious. In many ways a Princess is a product of a decision not to be something rather than a decision to be something. In fact, a Princess at the beginning of her journey might be horrified to think that she was on a path to become a wholly actualized and complete woman. Such an image of herself might be an incredibly frightening concept.

Instead the journey usually starts as the Princess-to-be decides that some condition in her life is much too confining. When a Princess decides to end a confining condition she has taken an irrevocable step forward toward creating her own destiny.

There are many steps in the journey before the Princess becomes conscious that she is on a path. She is simply making decisions to change her life, one at a time. Often she starts as a woman who has been taught that her self-worth is tied into serving others. She has never learned that her potential is unlimited and that she has the potential to rule as well as to serve. She does not start the journey thinking, "I am born to lead".

Her path begins by small acts of breaking away from her inappropriate training and any unhealthy expectations of others. At home it may be that she simply decides she is not going to cook dinner every night. Professionally she may begin to challenge the "old boy" networks. She questions the traditions and beliefs that bind her. As the small acts accumulate, she begins to understand that she is powerful. Each step forward is a struggle through some debilitating belief that has held her in place.

Each Princess has known pain and disappointment, some more than others. No Princess has allowed the pain to stop her. She learns through her struggle, if not by training, to value herself. She gives up all false gods and false guilt. She learns, sometimes the hard way, that pleasing others at the expense of her own dignity or health is an endless treadmill, destined to take her nowhere.

As she grows in her journey, the path begins to take a shape. She starts to recognize other Princesses on her path. She finds she relates to these other women better than the friends of her past.

Princesses are often recognizable by the fleeting evidence of past sadness in their eyes. These are not women who have simply accepted what was offered to them. These women are creating and they have often struggled for the opportunity to create.

As the Princess emerges from her cocoon, she finds herself compelled to join gatherings of other Princesses to celebrate the journey and the victories. These conclaves of Princesses become a time of sharing and of storytelling and ultimately of healing.

As she continues along her journey, these Princess gatherings become more and more important to her. They become an opportunity to share the more difficult or meaningful passages with others who understand and hold no judgments of her choices. She needs to talk to others who can help her remain objective about the many decisions facing a woman on a path to fulfill some destiny of which she is only vaguely aware.

Princesses have no images to uphold with other Princesses. They have given up the facade of "super woman" sometime on the journey long before they were able to recognize other Princesses. Their talks are blatantly honest in nature and refreshing to a Princess who needs honesty more than she needs adoration.

Each Princess is continually discovering that the more she values herself and treats herself as though she is of great worth, the more she is only attracted to others who hold her in great esteem.

As she grows, the Princess takes ownership as the creator of her life and, in doing so, she moves beyond her own expectations and often the expectations of others. Standards set by others for personal and professional development may no longer hold true and a Princess is very aware of this fact. Princesses have an acquired understanding of how power is really distributed in the Universe.

The Princess is always in transition. It is not that she is able to let go of all self-doubts. At times, she is overwhelmed by a fear of this path she is somehow compelled to follow.

Mysteriously, there is some inner system that keeps a Princess-to-be moving on her journey, keeps her producing in the face of adversity, and keeps her focused on some outcome that she cannot see.

The journey can appear chaotic. Only in retrospect, as the woman who becomes a Princess emerges, is it clear that she has continued over time to make a sequence of decisions that are a very straight path to a result far beyond what anyone might have predicted.

Sometimes, part of the journey of a Princess is to be betrayed or abused by those closest to her. Sometimes she does not achieve the successes she feels she deserves. Over time, she learns that these detours are just steps meant to redirect her journey. She learns to accept responsibility for everything occurring in her life and she learns to make wise and powerful decisions in the face of disappointment.

This ability to use adversity is the quality which separates Princesses from other women. She learns that only the Princess herself can polish her star until it shines so brightly that no one can deny its brilliance. No one can do it for her, and all Princesses know that this is true, even as Princesses help each other learn to polish.

When Princesses get together, they might laugh about whether it would be better to be a Queen than a Princess. And then they shake their heads, for one of their lessons has been to learn that rank is not always the objective.

"Who wants to be Queen?" one asks facetiously.

"Not me," they all say in unison.

Why not? It has to do with a construct about which each Princess is very clear. Princesses seek responsibility. They choose to lead by action and by example. They lead by guiding and showing the way. They do not assume any positional right of Leadership, but they earn their followers moment by moment.

Just as the title of Princess is arbitrary so is the assumption that being Queen is not the objective. A Princess (our Princess) has created a construct for the Queen as a ruler who sits in her chair and nods to indicate her wishes. Her right to lead is assumed by her position. Princesses want to differentiate themselves as leaders who guide rather than leaders who tell. They are perfectly capable of pulling rank and insisting on response when it is necessary, but they prefer not to do so.

An important lesson the Princess learns along the way is not to allow others around her to blame her for their choices. She has learned the hard way that she is the creator of her universe. She allows others to also take responsibility for the choices they make as well. She is not, nor does she have any interest in being an absolute Monarch if being so means that others abdicate the responsibility for the quality of their lives to the Princess.

Princesses become committed to living one very specific Law determining the life of a Princess over the life of an average woman. That Law is that they choose, daily, the experience of their own lives and that others do as well.

CHAPTER 3

PRINCESS POTENTIAL

Every woman is born with the potential to be a Princess. Not every Princess claims her birthright. The path is difficult and often confusing. There are so many detours designed to camouflage the pathway.

As children, there are adults in our lives who often have their own agendas for who and what we are to become. Those images are frequently fashioned by their own experience of what is possible. If we are very lucky, we are surrounded by adults who see our potential instead of their own limited stereotypes of what is possible.

These parents and teachers and friends rejoice in our cleverness, our wit, and our ability to create and to reason. Those who influence our self-image will see us as limitless in terms of our future. They will encourage our experimentation and our flights of fancy. They will not tell us what we cannot do, but instead will suggest all the possibilities. They will see no difference in our future than they see in the future of the most gifted and entitled of children, boy, or girl.

We all start the same. Prince or Princess, we are born with a brilliance that is evident in the face of any child. Perhaps the brilliance is our connection to our spiritual beginning, before we forget who we are.

Does that mean any child can be a Princess? Well, any girl child? (Princes have their own path to their potential.) The answer is unequivocally "yes" and there are well-known, well-loved Princesses in our cultures who have backgrounds that would hardly indicate the kind of mature and wise leaders they have become.

Because the young Princess-to-be sees the world through innocent eyes, she can be especially vulnerable. Insecure people are often drawn to her. Those who are insecure often have an insatiable desire to gain power over those who appear weaker in order to enhance their own sense of safety and comfort.

That is one reason why too many potential Princesses learn too early to reflect sadness. Those around them often don't know how to nurture the gift of the Princess. Instead they are threatened and find numerous ways to take the magic from the face of the child by asserting their use of control over her. There are so many ways to dim the light of a Princess. These are but a few:

◆ You can convince her that she is inadequate.

◆ You might tell her that she is not smart enough.

◆ You could assure her through your attitude or actions that she is unworthy of respect.

◆ You could simply tell her "how it is." She will believe you, whatever you say.

◆ Guilt is another way to control a potential Princess. Convince her that she is responsible for your happiness. She will believe you and she will grow up convinced that if others are displeased, it is her responsibility to fix it.

◆ You could show her through your own actions that the life of a woman is a life of sacrifice and denial.

◆ You could take the approach of teaching the young Princess about glass ceilings and the need to fight a constant battle for recognition.

◆ The most extreme way to affect a Princess's self-esteem is to abuse her physically. Nothing is more effective in teaching the young girl about her lack of worth. That lesson will stay with her for a lifetime, often coloring her expectations about life and love forever.

Many potential Princesses have been affected by one or more of the above examples. There are so many future Princesses out there who have been victimized by people perpetuating these myths and the behaviors that support them. It is very hard for a woman to overcome the lessons taught at an early age.

A Princess will emerge at the end of a long and exhausting journey, with her dignity intact. She will find her way through the many negative messages and will, in spite of the obstacles, become a powerful and distinguished leader. Her beliefs about her own potential will eventually come from her spiritual voice within and not from the limited imagination of others.

CHAPTER 4

PRINCESS DETOURS

The true Princess begins her journey on the day she decides that she really does not understand who she is and what she wants and that she must find those answers to thrive.

The path of a Princess is the path to self understanding. It is a journey of introspection and determination. On her journey, a future Princess will experience a multitude of detours, all designed to help her find her way. Those detours do not feel like gifts at the time, but in retrospect, almost every Princess will tell you that the detours were invaluable in helping to form the woman she has become.

There are many women who might look like Princesses to the untrained eye. They appear to have their lives well organized. These are the women who are educated, articulate, well-dressed, and in control. They have beautiful families, attractive, successful husbands, successful careers, but an emptiness in their expression that makes true Princesses walk past them without a second look.

Well, maybe a second look, but never a third. A Princess will recognize these women but she does not relate to them as Princesses. Many a Princess know these women and empathizes with them, for they remind the Princess of someone she once might have been.

Some Princesses *were* them a long time ago, before they understood that they were in fact being detoured from who they were supposed to become. Once, they too thought they had the world by its mythical tail, and did not know how much they did not know about how the world really worked. Once.

They also were not aware at that time how hard they were working to sustain the myth. They did not know how empty their relationships with their husbands and families really were. They worked hard to make the world believe they could do it all. They could manage their home lives and their professional lives with perfect style, perfect humor, and very little perception of their own needs.

These women who are now Princesses did not understand at the time that they were often living an old dream. The dream had little meaning for them, but it made everyone around them feel safe and even admiring of how well the future Princesses coped with so many responsibilities. The potential Princesses loved the admiration and worked hard to build the "Superwoman" image in the minds of others. She had no idea of the personal cost attached to the myth.

They did not understand that they had resigned themselves to a life of perfection that had no possible outcome other than their own destruction. They did not understand that they were building that life at a cost of their identity and personal fulfillment.

But, if it was their destiny to become Princesses, they eventually woke up. One day, they became so brittle from the demands on them that they either realized they could no longer perpetuate the myth of their perfection, or they simply ceased to function. Sometimes the realization that life was not working for them was enough to propel them forward into a search for meaning. And sometimes they just broke.

Regardless of whether the immediate outcome was a search for meaning or a breakdown accompanied by a verbalized or non-verbalized, "I QUIT!", the Princess-to-be families struggled with their rebellion. They frequently had no idea what was happening to their well-ordered lives. They had become so used to depending on the Princess-in-waiting's enormous dedication and energy, directed to *their* needs, that it never occurred to them that the circumstances might not be fair to this super woman in their lives. Why would it?

There is another group of women Princesses might recognize as they continue past them. These are the angry embittered women who have never felt that they belonged comfortably in any segment of society. Princesses now see that state as another detour from their potential selves. These angry women were taught early that they had no future and that lesson has been reinforced over time. Princesses see them, but they are not them. Some Princesses may have started there, too, but these women's lives hold no long-term interest for the Princesses because Princesses know that these women also have a way out. They know that these women make a choice to stay unhappy and that is one of the choices a Princess rejects at the beginning of her path.

Sometimes the women Princesses walk by are, in fact, healthy, happy, and content. If the contentment is not accompanied by a seeking and ambition to grow, the Princess will not recognize these women as other Princesses. In the Princess mind, growth is critical. Women who find their peace by allowing themselves to be dependent on and taken care of by others are not the Princesses described in these pages.

Once a woman decides that anger and bitterness are no longer serving her, or if she decides that she no longer chooses to live a life of meaningless perfection, the future Princess takes the first steps along a unique and challenging path. She realizes that she has been on a detour and she will start the journey back to the path that she was meant to follow.

Sometimes the journey begins with a crisis. Sometimes it starts with an introduction by another Princess. A word, a phrase, or a book can be the trigger. Whatever the starting place, the Princess will be drawn to all manner of tools that help her with her self-analysis.

Family and old friends may find her difficult to relate to. The detour she has been on is now a bumpy road filled with obstacles. She will often be teary or quick to anger. She will bury herself in herself and will sometimes want to talk about what is going on inside her. She will be drawn to other Princesses in various stages of the journey, for they will be the only ones who seem to understand.

She will no longer be available to others in the way she was in the past. Husbands often find the wonderful, agreeable partner they married is less agreeable. Children may find that she is not so available to their every whim. If they have been foolish enough to take her for granted, Princess families may feel the wrath she has kept to herself over years. The grievances the Princess feels and experiences at the beginning of her path are endless.

Once the Princess is on her path no one can intervene. To do so might incur great consequences to the spirit of the Princess and she will not allow it. Others can choose to accompany her or they can be left behind.

One of the things that will deter a Princess at the beginning of her quest is the initial reaction from her family. However, families should understand that, if the Princess's inner voice is strong enough, even the noise made by her family to bring her back to her senses will cease to control her. The Princess path is the path to shaking off all control other than the voice that calls out from inside her, trying to show the Princess her true destiny.

If the Princess is skilled enough in how she communicates with her family, she can help them to understand her journey. They may choose to follow her path with interest because they can learn from what she is doing. Unfortunately, because of the threat to their own status quo, the Princess often finds her family unsympathetic to her inner turmoil and to her need to pursue understanding.

Once the journey begins, frequently with a throwing over of 'what is', she will explore many avenues. The Princess will look at her life with a critical eye. She will dive deeply into purpose and into her own essence. She will often re-evaluate her profession. She will explore her personal style. Her dress and demeanor may change radically. Many times she will dive into scary (for others) spiritual studies including the paranormal and alternative spirituality.

Another bit of bad news: The journey back to her true self can be very, very long. It may start with self-help books, pass through therapy and a rejection of everything status quo, and eventually settle into a rhythmic examination of everything crossing the Princess's path. Once the quest begins, it never ends. The Princess is continually reinventing herself, integrating her new understandings into her personality. The Princess is in the process of creating herself according to her own newly forming beliefs, rather than the beliefs of those who taught her their "truth" in those early years where she assumed that age and authority meant wisdom.

Over time, Princesses generally reject their old addictions, whatever they might be. Addictions of any kind were more detours designed to hold her in place. As a Princess evolves, she finds drugs and alcohol less and less relevant to the inward journey she has begun. She will also reject old addictions to certain types of men who value her less than she has come to value herself. Each behavior that reflects an inner turmoil is sorted through and understood.

Eventually, the Princess learns to accept that the pain she experiences represents a powerful force to guide her along her path. She recognizes that the pain is a symptom that there is a belief controlling her response. She understands that her belief about the situation is what causes the pain and that the belief is a detour from her destiny. She learns to examine the pain closely to discover the belief in order to stay on her path.

Each restricting belief she uncovers frees her from the rigid binding of the past that locked her into a dance that was more about what others believed than what she herself wanted.

There may be moments during the process when the Princess asks herself if the journey is worth all of the pain. In fact, asking that question with all of the attending despair it may evoke, is sometimes a prerequisite to arrival at a Princess status.

One step at a time, a Princess heals the old wounds brought about by those who have filled her life and her understanding with misrepresentations. The depth of the wounds may determine the length of the process and the length of the detour.

What are the wounds the Princess must heal? How many layers are there to the onion? There are many types of wounds that must be sorted through, each woven among others, that determine the complexity of the path.

The only way to determine what must be healed is to start with the obvious sphere of pain and continually move to the next level. Her exploration of what is missing will be triggered by an inner voice indicating her unhappiness. The inner voice is the guide. When the voice becomes restless, it is showing the Princess where she must begin the journey and also saying that the journey must begin.

If her life does not feel full with meaning and if her life feels as though it is missing key pieces, then the odds are very good that the Princess needs to dive into and understand a belief system that keeps her from her bliss. The general dissatisfaction she feels may be a set of symptoms begging for evaluation.

For example, if the Princess feels unhappy in her marriage, she may start by trying to determine what is missing. She may have married a man who expected her to relate to him in a way that reflected what she believed the male/female relationship was supposed to be. Her outlook was created by what she was taught, what she observed, and, possibly, by what she was rebelling against. For example, if she had over-controlling parents, she may have chosen her partner because he was carefree and non-judgmental. He may have turned out to also be irresponsible.

A combination of elements created her beliefs about what she was looking for, and some of those beliefs were subtle enough that she was unaware of their influence on her choices. Now, as she searches for her own beliefs, she begins to identify the ones that are not helping her. She is moving beyond her original paradigm for choice.

Today, professional satisfaction also holds a major place in the evolution of the Princess. This added complexity may either enhance the growth of the Princess or it may create another layer through which she must sort. Generally, her professional life, or lack of it, helps the Princess to define her issues even more clearly.

The biggest driver of the Princess on her path is her need for freedom. The Princess seeks a level of freedom unattainable to those who turn away from the journey. She wants to feel totally whole in her skin, with or without anyone else in her life. She wants to feel secure in her place in the Universe. She wants to know she has worth that goes beyond anyone's opinions, positive or negative. She'd like to feel beautiful in her body and free to choose clothes that appeal to her, rather than to anyone else. She wants to be free of dependencies and she would like to never base her self-definitions on the success or status of her loved ones.

When a Princess has reached the higher level of her path, she needs no disguises. She has no one to impress. The only one at the end of the path for the Princess to impress is herself.

Depression is often part of the path to self knowledge. The depression may be a symptom that the Princess is in denial about a reality in her life. Whatever the hidden cause, when the depression consumes the Princess, it can also offer a diversion. The Princess hides from the tough choices she may need to make in order to resume the path for her own fulfillment by wallowing in the debilitating symptoms of the depression.

Her inner voice may be telling her she needs to build a life of her own. It may be telling her she has chosen the wrong career and she needs to start over. It may tell her she has picked the wrong partner or has given up too much of her identity in order to keep her partner. Whatever the cause, over time Princesses learn to recognize that the depression hides the thing the Princess does not want to face.

As you can imagine, staying on her path and avoiding new detours takes a lot of work. That's why a Princess is so recognizable. She has a demeanor no other woman has. She has a peace and a certainty about her that is different from those who have avoided the journey. And there is an elegance and a stature that comes with all the heavy-lifting. Vitality radiates from the Princess because she is truly engaged in her life. Why not?

CHAPTER 5

PRINCESS PASSIONS

All Princesses have one thing in common: They want it all. At any given moment, they are probably not going to be satisfied with parts of the picture. In fact, it seems as if they are never fully satisfied. If they attain the success they have talked about and dreamed about, they take very little time, if any, to examine how far they have come. Suddenly, the images shift and expand, and they see even more that they want to do.

Princesses set the goals high for their professional as well as their personal lives. They envision greatness as the outcome of their efforts, yet they assume that the vision is a limited statement of what they are capable of achieving.

If the Princess is running for office, why shouldn't she run for President of the United States? If she is working in an office, why shouldn't she be running the office? If she is managing a department, why shouldn't she manage the biggest department? If she is managing a company, why not the biggest company? Does it hurt the Princess to dream big?

Princesses don't think so and one way Princesses support each other is to encourage grandiose images.

Princesses are passionate about relationships... all relationships. They are particularly passionate about their love relationships. They believe they are entitled to the most elegant and sensitive of lovers. Single Princesses expect to find the perfect soul-mate as a partner and, as a rule, are quite picky. The partner is chosen long before the Princess actually meets him. She makes endless lists of qualities. He must meet every quality on the list to be considered for the commitment most Princesses long to make.

Married Princesses are never married just to be married. Remember, one of the steps along the path of the Princess is independence, both emotional and financial. A Princess believes that a marriage is meant to be a working partnership of equals. Such a partnership is difficult to attain because it reflects a perfect balance of strengths and weaknesses and a mutual respect that allows the two to create harmony where there might otherwise be chaos. The Princess is, by nature, a very strong personality. She chooses her partner to be the same. The two can sometimes create a tiny bit of friction as a result.

Married Princesses are as demanding of their husbands as the single Princess is of her prospective partner. She is passionate about their relationship and will never be satisfied with an easy and amiable relationship if there is no growth involved. In fact, the relationship is likely to have many passionate sparks if the Princess pursues her ideal relationship.

If a mate is incapable or unwilling to put the energy into the growth demanded by the Princess, he will find that she will lose interest in battling with him for what she wants. She will attempt to identify what is important many times, but there is a moment when she will observe that he is unwilling to change and that will be a defining moment for her. That is a moment that is very dangerous for the Princess' partner.

If she becomes apathetic or uninterested in the relationship because he has balked at continuing to grow with her, he should expect that she will begin to disengage from the relationship. The worst sign for a Princess' partner is when the Princess has stopped fighting. It means Princess has lost her passion for the relationship.

A Princess is never described as an easy personality. After taking the big steps along the journey, Princesses become more and more demanding. Perhaps demanding is the wrong choice of words. They become more and more expectant. They expect their professional lives to be filled with meaning and reward. They don't intend to be mediocre at anything and they don't allow anyone to treat them as if they are unworthy.

A Princess has passion for her work or she changes to something else. Passion is the core of who she is. Just as she doesn't marry to be married, she never works just to work. It is part of the vitality of the Princess to demand passion in every aspect of her life.

The Princess is passionate about her friends as well. A true Princess has very few social friends who do not fulfill a role in her evolution as a Princess. She does not seek friends just to have friends and she quickly eliminates people from her life who are not on a journey of their own. She has nothing to say to the others and small talk ceases to be satisfying somewhere after the first few steps on the path.

The Princess usually has a hobby or a

pastime that demands full attention when she is engaged in it. Perhaps it is one of the ways a Princess learns to balance her life. Many Princesses are part-time artists or writers. Some are deeply involved in sports. The specific activity doesn't matter. What matters is that life is both full and filled with things that have deeper meaning for the Princess.

Princess pastimes usually reflect an opportunity to continue to learn about herself and her needs. A Princess attacks nothing casually and is always looking for the deeper meaning in everything she does. If it does not involve an opportunity for introspection, she probably will not do it.

Being absorbed in personal growth is part of the reality of being a Princess. She is absorbed and consumed by herself and life. There is often a period when she first steps onto the path when her injuries and her awareness of them are so significant that all of her strength is devoted to their healing. This does not mean that she is not able to extend herself to the lives of others, but she is much better at doing so after she has healed the wounds of her misunderstandings.

The Princess's number one passion is

personal growth. A Princess's second passion is her family, however, on the road to becoming a Princess, family takes on a whole new meaning.

CHAPTER 6

THE PRINCESS FAMILY

Princesses have redefined the meaning of family. The Princess family is not always her genetic family. The family the Princess is born into does not always know how to nurture and grow a Princess.

To the Princess, family is "a way of being" rather than a right. Family is a behavior, not a bloodline. Family are those individuals who acknowledge our gifts, nurture our injuries, support us in our pain, and encourage us in our endeavors.

A true Princess always has a family. She will gather around her the kind of nurturing it takes to rebuild and support her understanding of the laws of the Universe.

Those who fit the definition are the ones Princesses want near them at the holidays. They are the ones Princesses call when confronted with sudden and frightening illnesses. Princesses gather their family together to celebrate their passages and their recognitions.

Family is defined as those individuals who

are unconditional about wishing the Princess success. Princesses have often struggled with the "family" members who have told them for years that they were not good enough, not smart enough, not ruthless enough, etc. to achieve their visions. Sometimes the genetic family members simply do not understand the Princess vision for herself. A Princess turns to other Princesses to sort out and overcome the negative voices in her head. They become each other's family with a set of rules that separate them from the dysfunctional behaviors of the average family.

There is no jealousy among Princesses. Those who act out of envy or negativity do not stay in the Princess family. They are quickly and elegantly dropped with unspoken agreement among the rest of the family members.

Princesses cease to have guilt about those who no longer fit the definition they have evolved for family. It is also the right of the Princess's genetic family members to be who they are, but if they are destructive in their interactions with others, Princesses are wise enough not to bring the vipers into their own den.

By the time a Princess defines her family and acts on her definitions, she has already paid a high price for healing. Some of the steps may have already been to allow genetic family members less and less access to her vulnerable spots. She has learned that the healthy response is not always the most popular response. But then, a Princess is not looking to be popular and she certainly has given up being perfect in the eyes of those who will always find fault with her.

As a Princess learns these lessons of family, her genetic family also has choices. If they choose to do so, they can operate within her circle in a healthy, productive way. She welcomes them gladly because she would always prefer to include them.

If individual family members need to continue demeaning and disrespectful behavior toward the Princess in order to feel good about themselves, an evolved Princess removes their opportunity to hurt her. She simply becomes unavailable.

A true Princess feels no obligation. For those who are needy in a draining way, she has distance. For those who are aggressive and attacking, she has walls that provide no access. For those who are reactive and disrespectful of her, she provides no opportunity. For those who are loving and kind and generous, she has endless capacity.

As a Princess becomes more respectful of herself, others become more respectful of the Princess. But even more significant is the fact that so many Princesses' offspring learn to be kinder to themselves as well. They don't repeat her path of needing to be 'perfect' at the cost of being happy.

Some of the first moves away from unhealthy relationships with Princess families were the most difficult. They were filled with guilt and uncertainty, but a Princess cannot stop what she has started. It is impossible and so she keeps moving. And sometimes the journey away is the very thing that brings the family back together.

CHAPTER 7

PRINCESS PARTNERS

Princess partners are important enough to deserve their own chapter.

Remember, Princesses frequently do not start their adult life knowing that they are Princesses and that they deserve to be treated as such. They often attract people as confused about themselves as the Princess is about her own self-worth. As a result of some very bad choices in partners, many Princesses have many disappointments along the path.

Many Princesses learned the skills of communicating their needs long after one or more important relationship has ended unfortunately. Not always. Some Princesses chose well early and are still with their first committed partner. To be a Princess however, the two will have grown through many stages together as the Princess has discovered who she is.

Princesses rarely hate their past partners. They grieve for the lost potential of the relationship. They miss the person they loved and the qualities that brought them together.

One of the reasons the progress is so very difficult for the Princess is that part of the journey involves taking responsibility for the things that have not worked out in her life. As she explores her failed relationships, she is overwhelmed with the sadness of what she has learned and the mistakes she made in the process of learning. She has no need to go back to the past but she also realizes that the failures were often caused by things that needed to be learned. "Will I ever get it right?" she wonders as she counts the lovers who were not meant to be.

The Princess' lover will evolve as she evolves. If she is lucky, she picks well the first time, and he grows and changes as she grows. If she is not lucky, she must discover what she needed to learn from the men she spends time with on the path to the right man.

She is looking for a true partner. A Princess does not spend time in frivolous relationships. She may try, but empty relationships always leave her drained and sad. Her friends urge her to have fun and not take men so seriously, but she is a serious woman. A woman with a casual attitude toward love affairs is not a Princess on her path.

There are many qualifications that must be

sorted through as she looks for her partner. He must understand her on all levels. A man who believes women to be less intelligent or less competent than men will never be an appropriate choice for a Princess. A man who cannot look in the mirror and see his own flaws will never pass the test of the most introspective of women.

She is looking for someone who knows her worth. A man who takes her for granted will soon find himself standing in the street looking at the closed door to her heart.

Once a Princess has determined that a man is wrong for her, she moves on. A true Princess learns over time to trust herself and to never look back with regret. Sadness perhaps, regrets never.

After enough (maybe one, maybe a dozen) failed relationships, a Princess becomes confused about what she thinks she knows. She has learned that her emotions are not to be trusted. The right partner may stand before her, and she may not recognize him.

By the time she meets her true partner she may have experienced all manner of betrayal from the men in her life. She has taught herself to know her own worth. Even though she has moved past a need to attract the kind of men she attracted in the past, she may be slow to realize that the man in front of her is not another lesson.

Trust is perhaps the biggest challenge for the man who decides that he wants a Princess for a partner. Princesses are not for the faint of heart. They are demanding and challenging and they trust slowly and conservatively. They have a history of seeing the potential in a man rather than the reality of the man and they have learned from their naivety. They want the pain to stop more than they want to be in love.

A Princess who has suffered and learned begins to demand what she has always hoped for in the past; respect. This woman feels too weary to make another mistake. She is challenging and intense about what she wants. She is often magic to a man who has been looking for a woman who knows her own mind.

As a result, not only is the relationship charged with energy, so is the man. He finds that just as he is expected to infuse energy into his Princess, so is he infused with her energy.

The Princess is quicker to know when it is wrong than when she was just a Princess-in-training. Woe unto the man who betrays a Princess. Her anger is swift and definitive. As a

Princess, she knows her worth and a betrayal is for those still learning the lesson of Self. If her partner underestimates what he has connected with, he will regret that lack of understanding. She has spent her time and paid her dues in attempting to salvage relationships with men who lost their heads and forgot they were tied to someone special.

In her past she may have taken full responsibility for the quality of the relationship. Before she had Princess friends and Princess family, she might have cried and pleaded and asked for understanding from the man who sold her out.

As a Princess, she knows better. It is not her responsibility to raise the man she has pledged herself to. He can go do his growing up with a non-Princess or a Princess-in-training who does not yet know her own worth. She is through with that.

When the Princess truly learns that she does not need the lesson of betrayal to learn what she deserves, she starts identifying with grown-ups who don't need to prop up their self-esteem by spreading their loyalties and affections around. Hopefully she learns it early because that is when the Princess comes home.

CHAPTER 8

THE PROFESSIONAL PRINCESS

Today more than at any other time, there is a place of leadership for women in the workforce. A professional woman can be found at all levels of our workforce with the criteria for "professional" being that she values the outcome of her work and takes it seriously.

When a professional woman becomes a Princess, everything changes for her. She goes from a woman who struggles to make herself heard to a woman who is confident and clear in her leadership. Others seek her out because she offers something unique and hard to define.

The Professional Princess is a product of her journey. She has learned about power and wisdom and she feels no need to compete for position. As a result, she refuses to be sucked into battle by those who are threatened by her confidence. She understands relationships and works hard to be responsible with her knowledge.

The Professional Princess understands that there is no such thing as a glass ceiling just for women. People will run into obstacles and biases anywhere. For every example of a glass ceiling in one organization, there is another example of an organization that promotes women to key leadership roles. No one has confined the Princess to stay where she is not valued.

The timing is right for the Professional Princess to evolve to her greatest potential. The world is more ready than ever before to recognize the female leader.

Today you will see Princess Professionals at the top of some of the most powerful male-dominated organizations in the world. What makes them unique? How did they get there?

If you study these women who have achieved positional power in traditionally male environments, you will find them significantly different from the stereotypical women's advocates who enter every opportunity for battle with weapons drawn.

These women recognize their value as women. They realize that they bring something different to the equation. They are undoubtably smart. They have a business savvy that separates them from the average person, male *or* female. And they have confidence that they do, in fact, have a contribution to make.

Rarely do these women need to battle head-to-head for power. They do not need to look and act like a man to get permission to produce. They are decidedly feminine in their dress and their behavior. Many of them take pride in their nurturer role with their families.

Not only do these women not apologize for their femininity, they often leverage it. In heavily dominated male situations, a women can often assert her presence and change the energy in the room. If she does not attempt to act like a man, her presence will often calm them and make them more thoughtful about what they actually say out loud.

Princesses have learned things about the world that are invaluable in business settings. They have evolved a belief system that allows them and others to be human. They accept and thrive in circumstances that others find impossible. They see opportunity in adversity where some individuals use the adversity as an excuse.

Princesses have already broken through the debilitating belief systems that would turn them into "yes" people in an organization. They lost the need for constant approval somewhere along the journey. As a result they are able to gain trust quickly in new situations because they are not trying to protect some impossible image of themselves. They communicate honestly and people feel the difference.

You can read about some of these women at the top every day in Fortune or Business Week or the Wall Street Journal. They have become "media candy" because they are vibrant and enthusiastic about what they are doing. They see the light at the end of the tunnel and they stand above their peers due to the sheer excitement they exude. In times when others are claiming competition or costs as the issues that keep them from success, the Professional Princess is finding new paths and identifying strategies that look simple in retrospect.

Simplicity is one of the strongest assets of the Princess Professional who suddenly is discovered and leaps to the top of these organizations. She arrives, she looks around, she listens and then she points. "Over here," she says calmly. And then she wonders. "Am I missing something? Why does this seem so simple?"

The reason is not so difficult to identify. She

has no false gods and no false guilt. She left them behind long ago on her Princess journey. It is much easier to identify and implement the correct solution when you are not trying to determine how to impress others. In fact, many individuals may have thought the same things that she says out loud. The answers were not so difficult. It was getting through all of the politics that presented all the problems. Fortunately, Princesses are never very good at politics. It doesn't fit well with the journey.

The Professional Princess is not trying to prove anything to anyone. She is trying to help. She does not need to teach others the lessons of humility. When she finds her progress stopped by some form of arrogance, she moves around it or finds an organization that values her performance and removes the arrogance of others as an obstacle.

Princess Professionals are different because they are not fighting a battle for recognition. They assume they belong in the board room and are often surprised and dismayed when they find themselves the center of attention because of the status they have achieved.

Princesses have learned that there is an order

to events. There are always the moments of give and take, and if the timing is right, a person can cause events to turn by a simple comment. Asking the right question in the right moment can completely change the most determined mind. Rather than being full of self-importance and demands that others pay them respect, powerful women know their own worth. Princesses have learned to be wise rather than aggressive with others. They focus not on the rewards, but on fixing the problems. They are confident that they will be rewarded in the right time, and they place little if any emphasis on personal recognition. They appreciate it when it occurs, but they do not seek it. They recognize that moment when those around them forget that they are women and accept that they are invaluable members of the team.

Powerful women in our work environment rarely feel that it is their duty to punish male ignorance. In fact, women who take on the burden of filing harassment lawsuits and other overt acts of battle often suffer for their bravery. There is a certain wisdom to understanding that it is not our job to be certain that others understand and are punished for their faults. A Princess understands that the laws of cause and effect will take care of every offense. Given time, the Universe is always more effective at teaching lessons than we could ever be.

For those ignorant men who attempt to assert their power over a Princess sexually, she has no patience and no fear. She has already learned that their behavior only demeans them.

The Princess chooses freely to stay only where she is valued and never bemoans the fairness of life or a situation. It is a waste of valuable energy.

It is relevant to study those successful women who have somehow broken through the "glass" ceiling. Do you believe it is possible that they somehow made it to the top without ever being harassed?

Hardly. But how did they get to the top? Ask them. You will find that they have a very cavalier attitude toward those awkward, demeaning moments that many women make a battleground. They treat males who can't figure out the boundaries with humor and disdain. They act as if the perpetrator is of no consequence, which indeed he is, unless the woman gives him consequence.

Rank and credentials have little meaning for her progression. She is often oblivious of credentials like education and work experience and, amazingly, the gates still open to her almost magically. The Princess just assumes that it is her destiny to be successful beyond reason.

Surprisingly, others learn to believe in her as well. Few question her ability to succeed, for they have seen her move through defeat as if it never existed. When a Princess runs into a wall, she simply goes around it.

The Princess Professional knows herself and has brought that knowledge to her work. She offers insight and wisdom where others offer cleverness and expediency. The world is ready for the Princess professional. In fact, the world may not survive without her.

CHAPTER 9

PRINCESS PARTIES

Princesses need to get together. They need to share their stories, their victories and their defeats. They need to get away and leave responsibility behind because their lives are filled with responsibilities.

They have chosen a difficult path and there are sometimes few opportunities for recognition along the journey. Frequently, as the Princess moves toward freedom, many are offended by how she is choosing to live her life. She is criticized and she is judged. But she is always learning. She needs events to mark her passage as she breaks free from their judgment.

It is, as we have said, a difficult path. The amount of courage it takes to confront yourself and your weaknesses continuously is amazing.

At any given moment you can find many Princess celebrations in progress. They aren't necessarily called Princess celebrations. There may be anywhere from three to fifteen women who have decided they need a getaway weekend and have left family and work behind to gather together.

Why are these weekend retreats popping up simultaneously with groups of Princesses who have never heard of each other and who may not know that they are Princesses? They are happening because that is often the way social movements occur.

These conclaves are happening any time of year and in any location. Location and weather are irrelevant. The common theme is the need to celebrate together among women who are taking extraordinarily courageous paths and who want to reinforce each other on the journey.

The Princess party is like a shot of adrenaline to help sustain the Princess on her path. There are some common themes to these parties.

The rules of the party are few. Spouses and children are courteously uninvited. The dress is casual, very casual. Some women take presents to their Princess gatherings. Usually the presents are some form of pampering for a fellow Princess.

Bring a Princess gift to pass and all your funny and weary stories of the last year, even if you have all heard them in your numerous telephone conversations. (Mostly Princesses live a long way apart because you don't find

Princesses all gathered in one place----they are rare, you know!).

Other than that, there are no rules.

Friday night is a reunion. Princesses laugh and cry and tell stories late into the night. They often explore their psychic ability and try to predict the future for each other. Princess gatherings will often experiment with paranormal concepts like channeling and using the intuitive to predict the future. Lighting candles and talking about destiny and the soul is often part of these events.

Princesses revel in their finding of each other. They wonder how they survived and grew so far into their potential without this extended and too precious family of Princesses? The first evening is always spent appreciating and caring for each other's wounds.

Princesses learned to do this. None of this was part of their training in pre-Princess lives. In the past, other women were the competition. Princesses had to dress better, look better, out-perform other women. Women's parties were events for feeling less significant and under the microscope. Not Princess parties. The guest lists are always carefully constructed.

Somehow, at a Princess Party, even when there are not enough beds, everyone sleeps peacefully. No one understands how or why. It must just be in the nature of the event.

Princess weekends are rarely about doing. They are about being together. You won't for example, find Princesses setting intense agendas for their time together. The weekends are allowed to unfold. This seems to hold true no matter what group of Princesses we are talking about.

Saturday morning, people move at their own speed. There is always someone ready to have coffee, ready to share that special story that is meant just for your ears. For whatever reason, Saturday morning coffee is the time when Princesses find there is someone special who has just worked through the lesson she is working on now, or who needs her experience on that particular lesson. Princesses talk and talk and talk when they get together, often not getting out of pajamas until the afternoon.

No one cares. No one worries about how they look. There are no masks to put on. Everyone moves around, conversation to conversation, talking and healing until they are full and satisfied with the healing energy they need to go back out into the world.

Sometimes Princesses do girl things like doing each other's make-up or doing group facials. They talk about clothes and decorating. It is truly a girls' weekend. They might go shopping or to a movie. Each choice they make is a choice to do what feels good at the moment.

Usually during a Princess weekend, Saturday evening is the true celebration. Some groups dress and go to a special restaurant. Others have dinners catered and pass presents. Never does one person cook. This is a weekend for resting and celebrating, not working.

Princesses will dress for the main event in whatever pleases them. Some need to dress up and others to dress down.

Sometimes Princesses try to include other women. Sometimes this works well and other times it is very difficult. What makes these groups of women work as well as they do is the fact that they have put down all their armor. They are authentic and easy with themselves. Women who come into the group are sometimes unfamiliar with the nature of a Princess gathering, and simply do not know how to respond. Occasionally, they are wary and full of pretense, which does not fit well in a room of Princesses who have long ago given up their defenses with each other.

Some Princess groups actually have prizes for the best stories of a Princess passage. Each woman must tell a story of an un-Princess moment in her life. There is a prize for the best story. Also, they can make up a story and there is a prize for fooling the most people.

Perhaps you can imagine the stories Princesses might tell. Or perhaps you can't. There is the woman who scaled the side of ship to get to her 'boyfriend of the moment', with the navy cheering her on. Sadly, the boyfriend didn't last, but the Princesses got the benefit of the story. There is the story of the woman who showed photos to all her co-workers of her prized Christmas wreath only to have it pointed out that there was a mirror behind the wreath and she was naked when she took the photo.

There are so many wonderful stories of women who are no longer embarrassed to laugh at themselves and laugh with each other at their all too human encounters with themselves.

Another element of Princess Parties is to share Princess routines with each other.

Princesses tell each other what they do in those special moments when they are honoring themselves and the beings they are creating. Princesses have learned to buy themselves jewelry and flowers and to take themselves to dinner to celebrate being a Princess between Princess Parties.

The Universe supports and revels in Princess decadence. The florists, on their own, begin to fill out the bouquets Princesses buy every week with the flowers they can no longer sell. Soon a $25 bouquet looks like a $75 bouquet as they fill in with slightly imperfect roses and other flowers the florists no longer feel they should pass on as premium. These flowers look totally perfect and somehow the roses open gloriously when they are sitting in a Princess vase.

As Princesses learn to honor themselves, they also find that they have attracted others who honor them as well. Princess stories are full of the people who have come into their lives in the present who are very different than the people who were in their lives when they began their climb. Their friendships are richer, their families more appreciative, their co-workers more respectful.

Princesses have gone through the looking glass to the other side, and they have gained enormously for their hard work. They have also learned that the time they spend together is the most precious gift they can give themselves. Sharing their stories reinforces a path that continually improves the quality of their lives.

CHAPTER 10

PRINCESS LAWS

The mature Princess lives by a set of laws she learns along her journey. Whenever she is faced with a dilemma, she accesses her understanding of how things work and attempts to apply those understandings to her life. The following are a set of laws to guide the Princess on her journey:

◆ A Princess's life is meant to be full of light and love. Nothing else is good enough.

◆ A Princess must listen to and trust her feelings. They are her only guides to her own joy.

◆ A Princess must not be afraid to stand on her own. Any dependency becomes, over time, a chain.

◆ A Princess should only allow people to be close to her who are supportive and nurturing. Those who drain her energy should be held at a distance.

◆ A Princess should honor herself. Presents, flowers, jewelry, and luxuries are appropriate.

Parties with other Princesses are a necessity.

◆ A Princess recognizes that her wisdom is needed. She feels no apology for stating her truths.

◆ A Princess chooses her equal for her partner. She only partners with those who also want to grow.

◆ A Princess understands that the Universe has a plan for her. She is patient with her losses on the way to claiming her destiny.

◆ A Princess is brave about facing what is not working in her life, even when the potential cost is great.

◆ A Princess is not responsible for fixing the world, but she is responsible for fixing her own world.

If you enjoyed <u>The Princess Way</u>, please check out these other books by Toni Lynn Chinoy:

In Search of a Yatz, a love story. In Search of a Yatz is a novel written for every person who has loved and lost and not understood. It is a weave of fantasy and reality that creates understanding about the most complex of human relationships.

Perfect Speed. Perfect Speed is a short book that helps the reader explore his or her own potential and the belief systems standing in the way of achieving the most exciting and fulfilling of possibilities.

The War Between the Whirligigs and the Tanks. This short book helps the reader understand and more effectively handle clashes between two distinct personality types. How does a Whirligig (the most free and risk taking of individuals) maintain respect and engage effectively with the Tank (the type of individual who is dedicated to planning and thinking through actions to arrive at the most safe and powerful of outcomes)? This text will help your work relationships as well as your personal relationships. *What to Do When It Rains, a handbook for leaders in crisis.* This book, as the title suggests, represents a full handbook which offers a model for leadership that is unique and extraordinarily helpful in addressing the complex issues facing leaders at all levels. The story which runs throughout the text, helps the reader identify with the principles and issues outlined in the content of the book by creating a real life example of the model in action. Many executives use this book as an aid in diagnosing and solving problems that plague their organization.

Coming soon: The second volume to the Leadership handbook entitled *What to Do When It Rains, a handbook for organizations in crisis,* will be out in the Spring of 2000.

Call us at our Harlan-Evans, Inc and Catapult Press headquarters at 540-668-7158 or contact us through toni@harlanevans.com